Fluõ | Travel

FUNCHAL

PORTUGAL

MINI
SURVIVAL
GUIDE

C000109960

Funchal: Mini Survival Guide
By Jan Hayes

Copyright © 2018, Jan Hayes. All rights reserved.
Edited and published by Fluo | Travel.

First Edition: July 2018

Scale / 1:7500

| ▬▬▬▬ 100m
| ▬▬▬▬▬▬ 500ft

Contains open data, licensed under the Open Data Commons Open Database License (ODbL) by the OpenStreetMap Foundation - © OpenStreetMap contributors.

While the publisher and the authors have used good faith efforts to ensure that the information and instructions contained in this work are accurate, the publisher and the authors disclaim all responsibility for errors or omissions, including without limitation responsibility for damages resulting from the use of or reliance on this work. Use of the information and instructions contained in this work is at your own risk.

No part of this book may be reproduced or utilized in any form or by any means, electronic or mechanical, including photocopying, recording, or by any information storage and retrieval system, without permission in writing from the author.

Contents

At a Glance

Country	Portugal
Region	Madeira
Native Name	Funchal
Established	1424
Language	Portuguese
Currency	Euro (EUR)
Plug Type	C, F (230V)
Driving	Right-hand
Population	111,892
Area	76.15 sq.kms
Postal Code	9000
Area Code	+(351)291
Timezone	WET (+0)
Timezone DST	WEST (+1)

ACCOMMODATION

 HOSTELS

Residencial Funchal ▷ 15 Rua do Hospital Velho 19A • Santa Maria ▷ 20 Rua de Santa Maria 151A

 HOTELS

Aparthotel Imperatriz ▷ 19 Rùa Imperatriz D Amelia 66 • Arts In ▷ 16 R. Conde Carvalhal 51 ☎ 00351291215290 • Avenue Park ▷ 19 Avenida do Infante 26D • Caju Boutique Hotel ▷ 19 R. do Surdo 1B • Castanheiro Boutique Hotel ▷ 15 Rua do Castanheiro 31 • Central ▷ 15 R. do Carmo 18 • Girassol ▷ 18 Estrada Monumental 248 ☎ (351) 291 70 15 70 • Hotel Bunganvilia ▷ 18 R. da Casa Branca 98 • Hotel Catedral ★ ★ ★ ▷ 20 R. do Aljube 5 • Hotel Jardins do Lago ★ ★ ★ ★ ★ ▷ 14 Rua Dr. João Lemos Gomes 29 • Hotel Madeira ▷ 19 R. Ivens 22-29, 9000-044 • Madeira Bright Star ▷ 19 Rua Princesa Dona Amélia 25 • Madeira Panoramico Hotel ★ ★ ★ ★ ▷ 18 R. dos Estados Unidos da América 34 • Madeira Regency Club ▷ 19 Rua Carvalho Araújo 9 • Mirasol Pensão Residencial ▷ 20 Rua Bela de Santiago 67 ☎ 291201740 • Molhe Apartments-Pina ▷ 15 R. Nova do Pina 10 • Monte Verde ▷ 18 Azinhaga da Casa Branca 3C • Penha França Mar ▷ 19 Rua Carvalho Araújo 2 ☎ +351 291 204650 • Pestana CR7 Hotel ★ ★ ★ ★ ★ ▷ 19 Av. Sá Carneiro 3 • Pestana Carlton Park ▷ 19 Rùa Imperatriz D Amelia 152 • Pestana Casino Studios ▷ 19 Rùa Imperatriz D Amelia 60a •

Pestana Village ▷ 18 Estrada Monumental 194 • Quinta Mae dos Homens ▷ 16 R. Mãe dos Homens 39 • Quinta da Casa Branca ▷ 18 Azinhaga da Casa Branca 1 • Quinta da Fonte ▷ 14 Caminho dos Saltos 68 • Quinta da Penha de França ▷ 19 Rua Imperatriz Dona Amélia 85 ☎ +351 291 204652 • Quintinha de São João ★ ★ ★ ★ ★ ▷ 19 Levada de S. João 1C • Residencial Americana ▷ 15 Largo do Chafariz 21 ☎ 291 215360 • Residencial Chafariz ▷ 20 Rua do Estanco Velho 5 • Residencial Monaco ▷ 15 Rua das Hortas 14a • Residencial Parque ▷ 15 Rua da Rochinha 17C • Residencial Pina ▷ 15 Tv. do Pina 12 • Residencial Queimada de Baixo ▷ 20 Rua da Queimada de Baixo 46 • Savoy Gardens ▷ 18 Azinhaga da Casa Branca 13 ☎ +351 291 213 600 • Sirius ★ ★ ▷ 15 Rua das Hortas 35 ☎ 291229357 , 291226117 , 291226118 • Suite Hotel Eden Mar Madeira ▷ 18 R. do Gorgulho 2 • The Residence ▷ 18 Rua de Leichlingen 9 • The Vine ▷ 19 R. Ivens 10 • Turim Santa Maria Hotel ▷ 15 R. João de Deus 26 • Vila Camacho ▷ 18 Beco da Amoreira 12 • Vila Lusitânia ▷ 18 Rua Fundação Zino 26 ☎ +351 291773603 • Vila Vicencia ▷ 18 R. da Casa Branca 45 • Windsor ★ ★ ★ ★ ▷ 15 Rua das Hortas 4c

EAT & DRINK

 BARS

Aqua Bar ▷ 19 Rua Princesa D. Amélia 18 • Açucar Doce ▷ 14 Estrada Dr. João Abel de Freitas Edifício Santa Luzia, Bloco 2, Loja E • Bar el Silencio ▷ 18 Estrada Monumental 191 • Bar o Mano ▷ 20 R. Bela São Tiago 39 • Barreirinha Bar Café ▷ 21 Largo do Socorro 3 • **Bom Sucesso** ▷ 16 Caminho do Meio 9 • **D. João** ▷ 15 Estr. Luso Brasileira 16 • **Dubaï** ▷ 19 R. do Favilla 5 • **Fx** ▷ 20 Calçada de São Lourenço 1 • **Harry's Bar** ▷ 19 Rùa Imperatriz D Amelia 69 • **Janota** ▷ 13 Caminho do Pilar 39 • **Madeira Rum House** ▷ 20 Rua de Santa Maria 241 ☎ +351 966 017 555 • **Mini Eco** ▷ 20 R. da Alfândega 5 • **O Avo** ▷ 20 Rua da Praia 49 • **O Garrafão** ▷ 20 R. Q.Baixo 40 • **O Nosso Bar** ▷ 19 Rua do Conde Cannavial 2 • **Pharmacia Bento** ▷ 20 R. dos Tanoeiros 4 • **Prá Poncha** (*sushi*) ▷ 18 R. Simplício dos Passos Gouveia 29 • **Revolution** ▷ 20 Tv. João Caetano 2A • **Scat** ▷ 18 Promenade do Lido 758 • **Sete Mares** ▷ 19 Av. Sá Carneiro 3 • **Tasca do Brazão** ▷ 13 Caminho de Santo António 79 • **Trap** ▷ 19 R. do Favilla 7 • **Venda Velha** ▷ 20 Tv. dos Escaleres 1 • **Victoria** ▷ 17 Estrada da Boa Nova 183A • **Vintage Bar** ▷ 20 Rua de Santa Maria 23

 CAFES

A Capelinha ▷ 15 R. Alferes Veiga Pestana 19 • **A Mercadora** ▷ 15 Rua do Hospital Velho 13 • **A Novidade** ▷ 15 Rua do Hospital Velho 9A • **A Preferida** ▷ 15 Rua do Hospital Velho 11 • **Afternoon Tea at Belmond Reid's Palace** ▷ 18 Estrada Monumental 191 • **Americana** ▷ 16 Tv. de São Filipe 23c • **As Manas** ▷ 13 Rua do Mercado da Penteada 13 • **Bar Consulação** ▷ 15 R. da Torrinha 53 • **Bar O Leque** (*regional*) ▷ 15 Praça do Município 7 • **Boutique Penteada** ▷ 13 Caminho da Penteada 36C • **Burger House Madalenas** ▷ 20 Rua dos Tanoeiros 56 • **Cafe Funchal** ▷ 20 R. Dr. António José de Almeida 6 • **Cafe de Praca** ▷ 20 R. do Esmeraldo 24 • **Café Vilar** ▷ 19 Rua Dr. Brito Câmara 9 • **Café da Fortaleza** ▷ 14 Beco do Amaro 39 • **Café del Mar** ▷ 20 Rua Dr. José de Almeida 5 •

Café do Museu ▷ 15 R. do Bpo. 19 • **Café do Teatro** ▷ 19 Av. Arriaga 45A • **Chaparro** ▷ 13 Travessa do Pico de S. João 8 • **Chave da vida** ▷ 20 Rua da Queimada de Baixo 29 • **Clube Motard da Madeira** ▷ 14 Rua da Carreira 240 • **Coca-Cola** ▷ 15 R. Hospital Velho 19A • **Confeitaria** ▷ 15 R. do Seminário 14 — 19 R. dos Aranhas 54 — (*coffee shop*) 20 R. Hospital Velho 4 • **Dinastia** ▷ 13 Caminho de Santo António 195 • **Fofinho** ▷ 15 Rua Dr. Fernão de Ornelas 55 • **Gelataria Mil Sabores** ▷ 15 Rua Dr. Fernão de Ornelas 10 • **Gelateria & Cafetaria Chafariz** ▷ 20 Rua do Estanco Velho 12 • **Grão de Farinha** (*sandwich, cake, coffee shop*) ▷ 15 Rua dos Netos 58 ☎ 291282062 • **Havaneza** ▷ 15 R. do Padre Gonçalves da Câmara 20 • **Kos Bar** ▷ 13 Av. da Madalena 146 • **Levada Nova** ▷ 16 R. do Acciaolli 13 • **Loja do Chá** ▷ 20 Rua do Sabão 33-35 • **Madalenas Café** ▷ 13 Av. da Madalena 98 • **O Verdinho** ▷ 20 Av. Do Mar 13 • **Padaria Doze** ▷ 14 R. de São Pedro 4 • **Penha D'Aguia** ▷ 20 Rua do Bispo 2 • **Penha d' agua** ▷ 20 R. de João Gago 4 • **Prince Charles** ▷ 14 R. da Mouraria 52 • **Quentinho** (*regional*) ▷ 15 R. João de Deus 2B • **Regiões House** ▷ 20 R. Direita 27 • **Rock & Coffee** ▷ 18 Rua Dr. Pita 21 • **Rosa Vermelha** ▷ 15 R. dos Netos 39 • **Saudade Madeira** ▷ 20 Rua de João Gago 2 • **Segredos da Casa** ▷ 19 R. dos Aranhas 72 • **Severa** ▷ 20 Rua Dr. Fernão de Ornelas 74 • **Snack Bar Flor do Pelourinho** ▷ 20 Largo do Pelourinho 23 • **Snack Bar da Sé** ▷ 20 R. Dr. António José de Almeida 6 • **Snack-Bar A Celha** (*regional*) ▷ 20 Largo do Pelourinho 33 • **Taberna do AVÔ** ▷ 15 Rua da Rochinha 96B • **Tea Room Alfazema e Chocolate** ▷ 20 Rua D. Carlos I 45 • **Tecnopan** ▷ 13 Caminho da Penteada 18C • **The Ritz Madeira** ▷ 19 Avenida Arriaga 33 ☎ +351291644166 • **Theos** ▷ 20 Av. Zarco 2 • **Uau Cacau**

(ice cream, pralines) ▷ 20 Rua da Queimada de Baixo 11

 RESTAURANTS

A Bica *(regional)* ▷ 15 Rua do Hospital Velho 17 • A Carreirinha *(portuguese)* ▷ 19 Rua da Carreira 77 ☎ 291223622 • A Morgadinha *(indian)* ▷ 19 R. das Maravilhas 80 • A Parreira *(regional)* ▷ 13 Caminho da Penteada 40 • Almirante *(regional)* ▷ 20 R. Casa da Luz 1 • Arsenal *(regional)* ▷ 20 Largo do Corpo Santo 26 • Asiático té Oriental *(asian)* ▷ 18 Estrada Monumental 318 • Bernini *(italian)* ▷ 19 Rùa Imperatriz D Amelia 66 • Casa Italia *(italian)* ▷ 18 R. do Gorgulho 11 — *(italian)* 18 Estrada Monumental 306 • Casa Madeirense do Funchal *(regional)* ▷ 18 Estrada Monumental 153 ☎ 291 766 700 • Casa Velha *(regional)* ▷ 19 Rua Imperatriz Dona Amélia 69 • Casal da Penha *(portuguese)* ▷ 19 Beco do Ataide 1 ☎ 291227674 • Castelo dos Hamburguers *(burger)* ▷ 14 Rua Da Carreira 306 ☎ +291 756 616 • Chalet Vicente *(regional)* ▷ 18 Estrada Monumental 238 • Colinas do Pilar *(mexican)* ▷ 13 Caminho do Pilar B • Do Forte *(portuguese)* ▷ 20 Tv. do Forte 3 • Dockside Bar *(international)* ▷ 19 Av. Sá Carneiro 3 • Embaixador Madeirense *(regional)* ▷ 20 Rua de Santa Maria 92 • Fora d'Horas *(regional)* ▷ 18 R. da Casa Branca 98 • Hamburgaria Do Mercado *(burger)* ▷ 19 Rua da Carreira 77 • Hamburgueria do Bairro *(burger)* ▷ 19 Av. do Infante 28d • Il Basilico *(italian, pizza, burger)* ▷ 18 Rua de Leichlingen 9 ☎ +351 291 708708 • Il Vivaldi *(italian)* ▷ 19 Largo das Fontes 24 • Indian House *(indian)* ▷ 19 Rua da Carreira 144 ☎ +351 291241653 • Istanbul *(turkish)* ▷ 19 Rùa Imperatriz D Amelia 101 • Jardim das Flores *(regional)* ▷ 19

R. Ivens 11 • Jardins do Infante *(regional)* ▷ 19 Avenida do Infante 56 • Jazz House *(regional)* ▷ 19 Rua dos Aranhas 16 ☎ +351 962844116 • La Pasta *(italian)* ▷ 20 Rua 5 de Outubro 5 ☎ +351-96-9960800 • La Vaca Negra *(steak house)* ▷ 18 R. Velha da Ajuda 13 • Latada do Doutor *(regional)* ▷ 15 R. Câmara Pestana 30 • Mania da Cozinha *(regional)* ▷ 14 R. de São Pedro 9 • Mercantil *(regional)* ▷ 20 Rua Esmeraldo 43 • Mercearia da Carreira *(snacks)* ▷ 19 Rua da Carreira 120 • Murças *(regional)* ▷ 20 R. Dos Murcas 83 ☎ +351 291 238702 • Nagoya *(sushi)* ▷ 18 Estrada Monumental 284A • O Chaparro *(Alentejana)* ▷ 15 R. João de Deus 3 • O Tasco *(regional)* ▷ 21 Rua Bela de São Tiago 137 • O piano ▷ 20 Rua de Santa Maria 98 ☎ 291222750 • PVP *(fish, sausage, regional, portuguese)* ▷ 18 Estrada Monumental 215 • Panoramico *(international)* ▷ 19 Est. da Pontinha 1-F • Papa Manuel *(italian, regional)* ▷ 18 R. Simplício dos Passos Gouveia 29 • Pinheira *(regional)* ▷ 17 Estr. da Camacha 99 • Pizza Caffé *(pizza)* ▷ 13 Caminho do Pilar 301 • Pomodoro Rosso *(italian)* ▷ 19 R. da Alegria 4 • Ratatouille *(italian)* ▷ 15 R. da Ponte Nova 16 • Regional Flavours ▷ 19 Rua da Carreira 146 ☎ +351 291 605 779 • Restaurante O Mesão *(portuguese)* ▷ 20 Rua dos Murças 13 ☎ 291220646 • Restaurante Pastelaria *(regional)* ▷ 20 R. Hospital Velho 4 • Restaurante Romana *(regional)* ▷ 20 Largo do Corpo Santo 19 ☎ 291 232 564 • Restaurante dos Combatentes *(regional)* ▷ 19 Rua de São Francisco 1 • Sabor da Índia *(indian)* ▷ 18 Rampa do Lido 8 ☎ 291765346 • Sabores Alentejanos *(regional, portuguese)* ▷ 14 Rua da Carreira 234 ☎ 291 758 406 • Santa Maria *(regional)* ▷ 20 Rua de Santa Maria 147A ☎ +351 291 649125 • Smart *(regional)* ▷ 15 R. do Bom Jesus 42

• **Solar da Ajuda** (*steak house*) ▷
18 R. da Casa Branca 102 • **Sum-
mertime** (*regional*) ▷ 18 Estrada
Monumental 219 • **Sunset Grill** (*international*) ▷ 19 Rua Princesa D.
Amélia 18 • **Taj Mahal** (*indian*) ▷
19 Rùa Imperatriz D Amelia 121 ☎
+351 291 228038 • **Taxiko** (*mexican*) ▷ 18 R. do Gorgulho 2 •
The Granny's House (*regional*) ▷ 18
Estrada Monumental 213 • **Touri-
galo** (*portuguesa*) ▷ 14 R. do Alto
do Pico B • **Trigal** (*italian*) ▷ 19 Rua
dos Aranhas 65 • **Viva Italia** (*italian*) ▷ 20 Rua Santa Maria 160 •
Xaramba (*italian pizza*) ▷ 19 Rua da
Carreira 67A • **Zarcos** (*regional*) ▷
17 Caminho da Igreja 19

EDUCATION

 UNIVERSITIES

Universidade da Madeira ▷ 13
Caminho da Penteada 16

ENTERTAINMENT

 THEATRE

Cine Teatro de Santo António ▷ 13
R. Coohafal C. R. L D

FINANCE

 ATMS

ATM ▷ 14 Rua Dos Ferreiros 272 —

18 R. Dr. Pita 2

 BANKS

BPI ▷ 13 Tv. Dr. França Jardim H3
— 15 Rua Dr. Fernão de Ornelas 44
— 20 Av. Do Mar 3 • **Banco BIC**
▷ 19 R. Conselheiro José Silvestre
Ribeiro 21 • **Bank** ▷ 20 R. do Sabão
61 • **Bankinter** ▷ 20 R. do Sabão 19
• **Caixa Geral de Depósitos** ▷ 13 Av.
da Madalena 99 — 20 Av. Arriaga
13 • **Deutsche Bank** ▷ 19 Av. do Infante 66 • **Millennium bcp** ▷ 15 R.
Câmara Pestana 11 • **Novo Banco** ▷
15 Rua Dr. Fernão de Ornelas 58 ☎
+351 291281846 — 19 Av. Arriaga 44
— 19 Avenida do Infante 46 • **San-
tander Totta** ▷ 13 Rua do Mercado
da Penteada 10 — 15 R. do Bpo. 5
— 18 Estrada Monumental 268 —
19 Bairro do Hospital Rua 1 9 — 20
R. do Aljube 14 — 20 R. João Tavira
30 • **Unicambio** ▷ 19 R. de São Francisco 2A • **Western Union** ▷ 20 R.
Dr. António José de Almeida 6

HEALTH

 CLINICS

Avasad ▷ 19 R. dos Aranhas 53

 DENTISTS

Clínica da Penteada ▷ 13 Caminho
da Penteada 41 • **Croma Clinica
Dentaria** ▷ 19 R. Ivens 28

 HOSPITALS

Casa de Saúde Câmara Pestana ▷
22 R. do Lazareto 125 • **Centro de
Saúde da Nazaré** ▷ 18 Av. do Colégio Militar 25 • **Madeira Medical
Center** ▷ 15 R. Hospital Velho 23A

PHARMACIES

Almeida ▷ 20 Rua João Tavira 39 • **Botica Inglesa** ▷ 15 R. Câmara Pestana 25 • **Confianca** ▷ 15 Largo do Phelps 15 • **Farmacia Avenida** ▷ 20 Av. Arriaga 2 • **Farmacia Central** ▷ 15 Rua 5 de Outubro 50 • **Farmacia Do Lido** ▷ 18 Estrada Monumental 207 • **Farmacia Dois Amigos** ▷ 15 R. Câmara Pestana 14 • **Farmacia Funchal** ▷ 19 Rua Doutor João Brito Câmara 48 • **Farmacia Honorato** ▷ 15 Rua da Carreira 58 • **Farmacia Nacional** ▷ 15 Rua Dos Ferreiros 47 • **Farmacia Portugesa** ▷ 20 R. Q.Baixo 2 • **Farmácia Bom Jesus** ▷ 15 R. João de Deus 12F • **Farmácia Bom Sucesso** ▷ 16 Estrada da Boa Nova 9E • **Farmácia Luso-Britânica** ▷ 15 Rua 5 de Outubro 81 • **Farmácia Morna** ▷ 15 Rua Dr. Fernão de Ornelas 23 • **Farmácia Nova da Penteada** ▷ 13 Caminho da Penteada 36A • **Farmácia Portuguesa** ▷ 15 Largo do Phelps 19 • **Farmácia Santa Maria** ▷ 20 R. da Boa Viagem 26 • **Farmácia da Nazaré** ▷ 18 Av. do Colégio Militar 25 • **Farmácia de S. Gonçalo** ▷ 17 R. Conde Carvalhal 205 • **Farmácia do Carmo** ▷ 15 Largo do Phelps 9 • **Farmácia dos Viveiros** ▷ 14 Estrada Dr. João Abel de Freitas 1

SHOPS & SERVICES

 MARKETPLACES

Mercado da Penteada ▷ 13 Rua do Mercado da Penteada 13

 POLICE

Comando Regional da PSP ▷ 15 Praça de Tenerife 30 • **GNR** ▷ 20 Av.

Do Mar 13 • **Polícia Judiciária** ▷ 19 R. Ten-Cel. Sarmento 17 • **Polícia Maritima** ▷ 20 Av. do Mar e das Comunidades Madeirenses 19

 POST OFFICES

CTT ▷ 13 Rua do Mercado da Penteada 11 — 20 Av. Zarco 7 • **CTT Santo António** ▷ 13 R. Dr. França Jardim 2 • **Correios** ▷ 15 R. do Arcipreste 7 — 18 Estrada Monumental 318 • **Correiros da Nazaré** ▷ 18 Av. do Colégio Militar 20

 SUPERMARKETS

Amanhecer ▷ 15 Rua 31 de Janeiro 68 — 18 Av. do Colégio Militar 20 • **Continente** ▷ 13 R. Dr. França Jardim 4 — 15 R. do Carmo 18 • **Curiosidades e Companhia** ▷ 16 Estr. da Boa Nova 11D • **Fruta e verduras** ▷ 14 R. Nova da Quinta Deão 39 • **Frutaria Bom Sucesso** ▷ 16 Estr. da Boa Nova 15C • **La Vie** ▷ 19 R. da Ponte de São Lázaro 3 • **Meu Super** ▷ 18 R. da Casa Branca 32A — 19 Av. do Infante 62 — 19 R. Cónego Jerónimo Dias Leite 5, 9000-052 • **Pingo Doce** ▷ 13 Rua do Mercado da Penteada 15 — 15 Rua Doutor Fernão de Ornelas 73 ☎ 351291209380 — 18 Estrada Monumental 1B — 19 Dr.João Brito Câmara 12 • **Spar** ▷ 18 Estrada Monumental 268 • **Super Rio Mar** ▷ 16 Estr. da Boa Nova 13 • **Supermercado Regional** ▷ 14 R. Cidade do Cabo 10

TOURISM

 ATTRACTIONS

Mosquito ▷ 20 Rua D. Carlos I 33A

• **Parrot** ▷ 19 Av. do Infante 1 • **Pelourinho do Funchal** ▷ 20 Largo do Pelourinho 1 • **Portas da Cidade** ▷ 20 Largo dos Varadouros 4 • **Steamroller John Fowler & Co.** ▷ 19 Av. do Infante 1

 ## INFORMATION

Jardim Municipal ▷ 19 R. Conselheiro José Silvestre Ribeiro 21 • **Pestana** ▷ 18 Estrada Monumental 189 • **Reception** ▷ 19 Rua Princesa D. Amélia 24 • **Tourist Information** ▷ 18 Estrada Monumental 284 — 20 Av. Arriaga 12

 ## MUSEUMS

Casa Museu Frederico de Freitas ▷ 14 Calçada de Santa Clara n°7 • **Instituto do Vinho da Madeira** ▷ 15 Rua 5 de Outubro 77 • **Madeira Optics Museum** ▷ 14 Rua das Pretas 51 • **Museu CR7** ▷ 19 Av. Sá Carneiro 3 • **Museu Henrique e Francisco Franco** ▷ 15 R. Alferes Veiga Pestana 19 • **Museu João Carlos Abreu** ▷ 14 Calçada do Pico 4 • **Museu a Cidade do Acúcar** ▷ 20 Praça do Colombo 5 • **Museu da Quinta das Cruzes** ▷ 14 Calçada do Pico 1 • **Museu de Arte Sacra** ▷ 15 Rua do Bispo 21 • **Núcleo Museológico da Madeira Wine** ▷ 20 Av. Arriaga 12 • **Núcleo Museológico do IBTAM - Museu do Instituto do Bordado e Tapeçaria da Madeira** ▷ 15 Rua Do Visconde De Anadia 44

 ## RELIGIOUS

Capela de Nossa Senhora da Oliveira ▷ 20 Rua de Santa Maria 50 • **Capela de São Luís de Tolosa** ▷ 15 R. do Bpo. 18 • **Capela de São Paulo** ▷ 14 Rua da Carreira 284 • **Convento de Santa Clara** ▷ 14 Calçada de Santa Clara 15 • **Igreja Jesus Cristo Santo Últimos Dias** ▷

19 R. Ten-Cel. Sarmento 25 • **Igreja do Carmo** ▷ 15 Largo do Phelps 13 • **Igreja do Socorro** ▷ 21 R. do Asp. Mota Freitas G 1 • **Nª Srª da Consulação** ▷ 15 R. da Torrinha 63 • **Salão do Reino das Testemunhas de Jeová** ▷ 13 R. da Levada dos Barreiros 8

TRANSPORT

 ## BICYCLE RENTALS

Happy Bikes ▷ 19 R. da Penha de França 3

 ## CAR RENTALS

Atlantic Rent A Car ▷ 18 R. da Casa Branca 47 • **Avis** ▷ 19 Av. do Infante 33 • **Europcar** ▷ 18 Estrada Monumental 175-B • **Futuro** ▷ 18 Estrada Monumental 268 • **Futuro Rent a Car** ▷ 19 Av. do Infante 62A ☎ +351 291 220721 • **Hertz** ▷ 18 Estrada Monumental 284A • **MADpoint** ▷ 18 Estrada Monumental 213 • **Renault Rent** ▷ 19 R. do Favilla 11 • **Rodavante** ▷ 18 Estrada Monumental 306 • **Sixt** ▷ 18 Estrada Monumental 137 ☎ +351-255788199 • **Wind car rent** ▷ 18 Estrada Monumental 306

 ## FUEL STATIONS

BP ▷ 13 R. da Levada do Cavalo 45 — 14 Rúa Arcebispo Dom Aires 3D — 15 Entrada N°79 3 • **GALP** ▷ 14 Rua de S. João 33A — 15 R. do Matadouro 12 — 19 R. do Infante Santo 1

 STATIONS

S.A.M. ▷ 19 Av.   Calouste Gul-benkian 900 • **SAM** ▷ 20 Av. Do Mar 13

Map   11

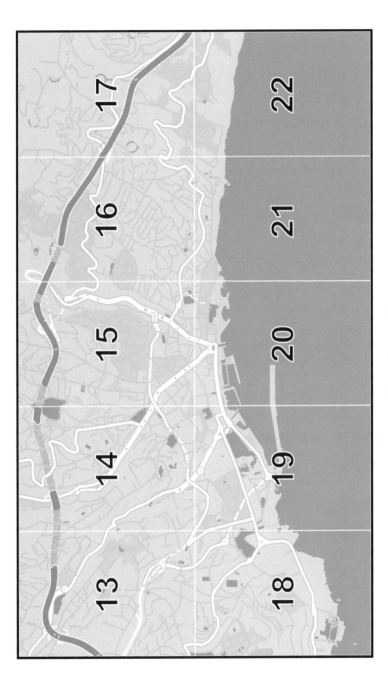

Map Overview

Archaeological site		Information
Artwork		Jewish synagogue
Atm		Kiosk
Bar		Library
Bicycle rental		Lighthouse
Biergarten		Memorial
Buddhist temple		Monument
Bus station		Museum
Bus stop		Muslim mosque
Cafe		Parking
Camping site		Peak
Car rental		Pharmacy
Cave entrance		Picnic site
Chalet		Playground
Church / Monastery		Police
Cinema		Post office
Courthouse		Prison
Department store		Pub
Drinking water		Railway
Dry cleaning		Restaurant
Embassy		Shinto temple
Fast food		Sikh temple
Ferry terminal		Sports centre
Fire station		Supermarket
Fountain		Taxi
Fuel		Telephone
Golf course		Theatre
Hindu temple		Toilets
Hospital		Townhall
Hostel		Traffic signals
Hotel		Windmill

Travessa do Pomar

Vereda Bela Vista

Jardim Botânico

Choreographed
Gardens
Hibiscus

Caminho do Meio

Palm Trees

Travessa do Transval

Beco do

Caminho da Lindinha

Bom Sucesso

Caminho do Meio

Rua Cabeço Ferro

Rua das Amoreiras

Estrada do Visconde Cacongo

Caminho da Casa Velha

Rua das Murteiras

Boa Nova

J.F. de Sa
Maria M

Largo São
João Bosco

Entrada da Porta de Ferro

Rua do Alto

Caminho do P

Rochinha

Rua Cidade de Maui

Rua da Pedra Suna

Rua do Faial

Rua do Rio de Janeiro

Ladeira do Farrobo de Baixo

Rua Conde Carvalhal

Chão da Loba

Rua do Agr

21

Jardim

Rua dos Salões

Ladeira da Fonte

Transval

Beco da Doca

Rua da Boa Nova

Caminho do Palheiro

Palmeira

Estrada do Aeroporto

Estrada da Car

Estrada da Pinheira

Centro
de Inspecções
da Madeira

Estrada do Aeroporto

o Palheiro

CANTO DO MURO

Rua Carlos Maria dos Santos

Rua Tenente Domingos João Cardoso

Rua da Pica de Pau

Estrada da Camacha

Estrada do Aeroporto

Bica de Pau

Rua do Serrado

Rua Conde Carvalhal

Caminho da Bica de Pau

Beco do Carteiro

22

Igreja

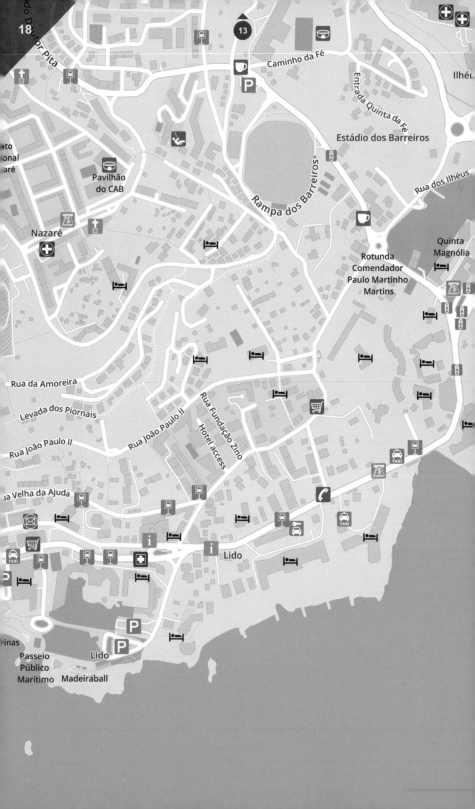

13

Caminho da Fé

Entrada Quinta da Fé

Ilhéu

Estádio dos Barreiros

Rua dos Ilhéus

Pavilhão
do CAB

Rampa dos Barreiros

Quinta
Magnólia

Nazaré

Rotunda
Comendador
Paulo Martinho
Martins

Rua da Amoreira

Levada dos Piornais

Rua Fundação Zino

Rua João Paulo II

Rua João Paulo II

Hotel access

Rua Velha da Ajuda

TAXI

TAXI

Lido

i

i

Lido

P

P

Passeio
Público
Marítimo

Lido

Madeiraball

inas

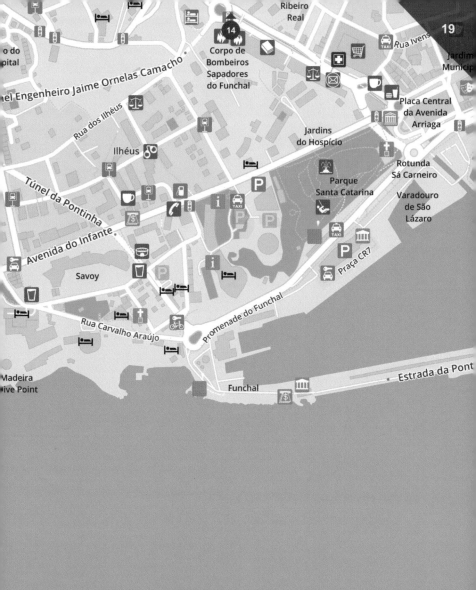

Ribeiro
Real

Corpo de
Bombeiros
Sapadores
do Funchal

Rua Ivens

Jardim
Municip

l Engenheiro Jaime Ornelas Camacho

Rua dos Ilhéus

Placa Central
da Avenida
Arriaga

Ilhéus

Jardins
do Hospício

Rotunda
Sá Carneiro

Túnel da Pontinha

Parque
Santa Catarina

Varadouro
de São
Lázaro

Avenida do Infante

Praça CR7

Savoy

Rua Carvalho Araújo

Promenade do Funchal

Madeira
ive Point

Estrada da Pont

Funchal

Edifício
do Governo
20
Regional
da Madeira

SÉ

Chafariz

Largo da
Restauração

Largo do
Pelourinho

Largo dos
Varadouros

Mercado
dos Lavradores

ZONA VELHA

15

Praça do
Povo

Jardim
Almirante
Reis

Prai
São

Cais do Funchal

Estrada da Pontinha

Louros

LAZARETO

Lazareto

Rua do Lazareto

Largo do
Socorro

rreirinha

Pedra Mole

Rua Nova da

Bairro de S. Gonçalo

17

Rua do Lazareto

Rua do Lazareto

Rua do Lazareto

BASICS

Hello

Oi
ˈoj

Good morning

Bom dia
bˈõ dˈiɐ

Good evening

Boa tarde
bˈoɐ tˈaɾdɨ

How are you?

Tudo bem?
tˈudu bˈẽj̃?

Fine, thank you

Bem, obrigado/a
bˈẽj̃, obɾiɡɐdˈɔ/ɐ

What is your name?

Como se chama?
kˈɔmu sɨ ʃˈɐmɐ?

My name is _____

Meu nome é _____
mˈew nˈɔmɨ ˈɛ

Nice to meet you

Muito prazer
mˈũjtu pɾɐzˈeɾ

Please

Por favor
puɾ fɐvˈoɾ

Thank you

Obrigado/a
obɾiɡɐdˈɔ/ɐ

You're welcome

De nada
dɨ nˈadɐ

Yes

Sim
sˈĩ

No

Não
nˈẽw̃

Excuse me

Desculpe-me
diʃkuɫpˈɛmɨ

I'm sorry

Desculpe
diʃkˈuɫpɨ

Goodbye

Adeus
ɐdˈewʃ

I can't speak ____ [well]

Não falo [bem] português
nˈẽw̃ fˈalu [bˈẽj] puɾtugwˈeʃ

Do you speak English?

Fala inglês?
fˈalɐ ĩglˈeʃ?

I don't understand

Não compreendo
nˈẽw̃ kõpɾiẽd

PROBLEMS

Help!

Socorro!
sukˈɔʀu!

Police!

Polícia!
pulˈisiɐ!

I'm lost

Estou perdido/a
ʃtˈo piɾdidˈɔ/ɐ

Can I use your phone?

Posso usar o seu telefone?
pˈɔsu uzˈaɾ ˈɔ sˈew tilifˈonɨ?

NUMBERS

1

um
ũˈ

2

dois
dojs

3

três
tɾˈeʃ

4

quatro
kwˈatɾu

5

cinco
sˈĩku

6

seis
sɐjs

7

sete
sˈɛtɨ

8

oito
ˈojtu

9

nove
nˈɔvɨ

10

dez
dˈɛʃ

20

vinte
vˈĩtɨ

30

trinta
trˈĩtɐ

40

quarenta
kwɐɾˈẽtɐ

50

cinqüenta
sĩkˈẽtɐ

60

sessenta
sɨsˈẽtɐ

70

setenta
sɨtˈẽtɐ

80

oitenta
ojtˈẽtɐ

90

noventa
nuvˈẽtɐ

100

cem
sˈẽj̃

1000

mil
mˈił

DAYS

today

hoje
ˈɔʒɨ

yesterday

ontem
ˈõtẽj̃

tomorrow

amanhã
ɐmɐɲˈɐ̃

Monday

segunda-feira
sɨɡũdɐfˈejɾɐ

Tuesday

terça-feira
tirsɐfˈejrɐ

Wednesday

quarta-feira
kwɐrtɐfˈejrɐ

Thursday

quinta-feira
kĩtɐfˈejrɐ

Friday

sexta-feira
siʃtɐfˈejrɐ

Saturday

sábado
sˈabɐdu

Sunday

domingo
dumˈĩgu

MONTHS

January

Janeiro
ʒɐnˈejru

February

Fevereiro
fivirˈejru

March

Março
mˈarsu

April

Abril
ɐbrˈił

May

Maio
mˈaju

June

Junho
ʒˈuɲu

July

Julho
ʒˈuʎu

August

Agosto
ɐgˈoʃtu

September

Setembro
sitˈẽbru

October

Outubro
otˈubru

November

Novembro
nuv'ẽbɾu

December

Dezembro
diz'ẽbɾu

COLORS

black

preto
pɾ'ɛtu

white

branco
bɾ'ẽku

red

vermelho
viɾm'ɐʎu

green

verde
v'ɛɾdɨ

blue

azul
ɐz'uɫ

yellow

amarelo
ɐmɐɾ'ɛlu

orange

laranja
lɐɾ'ẽʒɐ

LODGING

Do you have any rooms available?

Tem quartos disponíveis?
t'ẽj kw'aɾtuʒ diʃpun'ivɐjʃ?

I will stay for _____ night(s)

Ficarei _____ noite(s)
fikɐɾ'ɐj ___ n'ojtɨ(s)

I want to check out

Quero fazer o registo de saída
k'ɛɾu fɐz'eɾ 'o ʁiʒ'iʃtu dɨ sɐ'idɐ

MOVING AROUND

How much is a ticket to _____?

Quanto custa uma passagem para _____?
kw'ẽtu k'uʃtɐ 'umɐ pɐs'aʒẽj pɐɾɐ ___?

One ticket to _____, please

Uma passagem para _____, por favor
ˈumɐ pɐsˈaʒɐ̃j pɐɾɐ ___, puɾ fɐvˈɔɾ

How do I get to _____?

Como vou _____?
kˈomu vˈo ___?

...the train station?

...à estação de trem?
...ˈa ʃtɐsˈɐ̃w̃ di tɾˈɐ̃j?

...the bus station?

...à estação de ônibus?
...ˈa ʃtɐsˈɐ̃w̃ di ˈonibuʃ?

...the airport?

...ao aeroporto?
...ɐu ɐiɾupˈɔɾtu?

EATING

Can I look at the menu, please?

Posso ver o cardápio, por favor?
pˈɔsu vˈeɾ ˈɔ kɐɾdˈapiu, puɾ fɐvˈɔɾ?

I would like _____

Quero _____
kˈɛɾu ___

SHOPPING

How much is this?

Quanto custa?
kwˈɐ̃tu kˈuʃtɐ?

expensive

caro
kˈaɾu

cheap

barato
bɐɾˈatu

I don't want it

Não quero
nˈɐ̃w̃ kˈɛɾu

OK, I'll take it

OK, eu levo
ˈɔ, ˈew lˈɛvu

27209310R00020

Printed in Great Britain
by Amazon